250 Recommendations for Young Sales Agents

250 Recommendations for Young Sales Agents

Guide for Professional Conduct

Iulius Grosu

To order additional copies of this book, contact:
Xlibris Corporation
0-800-644-6988
www.xlibrispublishing.co.uk
Orders@xlibrispublishing.co.uk
300609

Contents

Introduction 7

I.   The qualities of a sales agent... 9

II.   Professional preparation 13

III. The instruments of a sales agent, attitude and
      few suggestions related to the working manner................................ 16

IV. The relation with your interlocutors................................. 24

V.   What not to do 29

VI. Instead of bibliography... 49

Introduction

The idea to conceive this material came to my mind a long time ago and has become more and more clear while, searching in libraries, I did not find any similar paper for young sales agents. We all know how hard it is to start without a minimum level of knowledge, without a directing guide to show us the correct manner of working and to protect us from the greatest enemy: the failure.

The most hidden desire I have is that, in the foreseeable future, the word *salesperson* become generally valid in the list of agreed professions in the true sense of the word and be recognized anywhere in the world. I insist on this aspect because I am convinced that each one of you have met at least once with the situation in which, in one way or another, different persons have spoken tendentiously about this profession. The ones who commit this mistake do not know how hard and how beautiful is the profession I refer to. And I say this especially because irrespective of the position held, from *Sales Representative* to *Sales Manager*, we all are SALESPERSONS!

I have started to sketch this content from the first day of 2006, a day with two very significant meanings, and namely: that year I turned 35 and 15 years in the field of sales. Each place in which I have worked has meant a new experience, another stage. As much as I could I have tried to avoid making previous mistakes. In most cases

I have succeeded, but I made other mistakes. Each time I learnt more both quantitatively and qualitatively. Thinking of what I have done all these years, I have realized that a great part of the knowledge I have come rather from personal observations and perceptions on the situations met that from a series of courses and trainings held in an organized environment. Following this retrospective, this question came to me very naturally: What would have been my level of knowledge and what would have been my current professional stage if I had benefited from a rigorous training system? It's hard to say. It is certain that my development process would have been much shorter.

This is the main reason which determined me to write this paper, which is not by far a solution of *modus vivendi*; nevertheless, I hope from all my heart that it is concise and coherent enough to offer young sales agents few advices in relation to a healthy and good sense modality to develop their activity. As I have mentioned from the title and as you will observe from the content, the material does not offer a "perfect" solution to achieve professional success, but draws the attention on many severe and frequent mistakes which appear in the sale action. That is why the last chapter entitled "What not to . . ." is more consistent than others. In conclusion, if you will hope that you will find the key for success in these lines, you will be deeply disappointed. In exchange, if you will read this paper with the clear intention to learn how to stay away from troubles, there is the possibility to find enough tips to eliminate mistakes and unpleasant surprises. Good luck!

I

The qualities of a sales agent

Each of you is gifted with qualities and defects; nothing spectacular in this affirmation. According to the specificity, each profession requires native or acquired qualities; all these can be perfected provided that the perfecting methods are the correct ones. Develop your qualities and diminish your defects! You will not succeed in total, but make constant and continuous efforts in this sense!

I.1 *Self-knowledge* - I consider that this is the most important quality of a sale agent. This quality enables you to know your own limits, pluses and minuses. By performing a correct evaluation and by knowing your real potential, you will be able to eliminate the barriers which impede you to develop. More than this, you must do this if you want to have notable results of performances; it depends only on you and on what you have proposed or want to do.

I.2 *Calm* - The act of selling is, besides the fight between characteristics and benefits, arguments and "pressing", a psychological confrontation between the two interlocutors; the one who gets nervous the first makes mistakes more often having thus the greatest chances to lose. Thus, in order to win, keep your calm, no matter what!

I.3 *Correctness* - It is very important to be correct, both with you and with the ones with whom you interact. With time, you will create a reputation of a correct and trustful person. This is one of the basic coordinates of the future relation. Not only for the image, but because it is good and correct to be correct! It will bring only benefits to you and to your career.

I.4 *Creativity* - It is an essential quality in this field. Except for the basic skeleton consisting of strategy and rules, each selling action is unique because it is different. That is why the work in this field is so nice—supposes a deep and continuous search for new arguments, methods and tricks. Be creative!

I.5 *Courage* - You must always use your courage to support (with arguments) your point of view in the situation in which you are firmly convinced that you are right. Attention: if you are not right, if you do not have solid arguments or if you do not have the ability and the training to use these arguments, the courage will be transformed in cheap and hilarious heroism.

I.6 *Determination* - Working in this field is not easy. The person who thinks the contrary has never worked in this field even for one day. That is why you must be continuously decided to go on with the chosen road and to be able to make efforts in this sense.

I.7 *Ethics* - It is an extremely complex concept and studied very intensely by specialists with rigorous limitations but also with a multitude of valences from other fields. What I know for sure is that this concept determines and defines the difference between professionals and the others.

I.8 *Initiative* - Without initiative, no action has any chances of success; this applies more to the sale activity which is a complex and long-time process.

I.9 *Trust* - Have trust in your own forces! Only in this way you will be able to achieve the objectives proposed! Still, there is an amendment: trust cannot be blind, but must have solid fundament.

I.10 *Loyalty* - Be loyal to your principles and objectives! Be loyal to the company you work in even to the last moment of your collaboration!

I.11 *Modesty* - This quality is specific to valuable people and to people of great value. Leave the persons around you with whom you interact to formulate opinions in relation to your performances, professionalism and attitude! This recommendation is not valid for the situations in which you are required by the specificity of the situation to emphasize you strengths!

I.12 *Optimism* - When you pass through difficult moments do not let the desperation restrain you. In these moments, your most valuable allied is optimism. Optimism will help you to launch again more powerful, more experimented and with a stronger desire to affirm.

I.13 *Order* - The lack of order in your activity and especially in your way of thinking is very dangerous. It affects your state, weakens your concentration power and implicitly reduces your capacity. Be efficient by order and discipline.

I.14 *Organization* - The organization supposes the existence of a rigorous system of criteria to filter and prioritize the activities, eliminating thus dead moments and unimportant or unproductive actions. The correct organization of the activity leads automatically to an increase of the performances. It is a necessary condition but not a sufficient one.

I.15 *Perseverance* - Be consequent and perseverant in your actions, both in those related by your work and in those related to your own training. This is the only correct and healthy manner which determines the professional maturing.

I.16 *Professionalism* - All your actions and your entire attitude must show professionalism, but not only at declarative level but also at the level of facts. In this way you will appear in front of everybody and you will differentiate from other sales agents. It is the separation limit between very good agents and the others.

I.17 *Punctuality* - Respect yourself and your interlocutors, respecting in this way everybody's time. If your interlocutor is not punctual, the fact that you have arrived in time to your meeting will make him feel inferior. You have an advantage you can use. Thus, be punctual!

I.18 *Patience* - Patience is a great virtue. With patience you will exceed difficult moments and situations and you will cross the stages of personal and professional development!

I.19 *Realism* - More important than optimism is realism. It is vital to evaluate correctly your chances and possibilities. In this way you will avoid over-evaluations which are so dangerous generating major mistakes.

I.20 *Responsibility* - You must always assume the responsibility of your actions irrespective if they are good or bad, but especially if you have committed a mistake!

I.21 *Seriousness* - This quality certainly had several valences; the moment you have been classified as a serious person, you have cleaned your path towards winning the trust of your interlocutors, the foundation stone of a sales agent (after knowledge): inter-human relations. Otherwise, the situation is tragic and you will have an enormously work to do in order to arrive to the previous stage.

II

Professional preparation

II.1 I want to ask you not to feel a complex due to the fact that you are at the beginning of the road and your level of knowledge is not a rich one. Nobody was born knowing! Think about all the persons who have arrived to a certain level of preparation and professional performance and were at a certain moment at the beginning. By means of hard work and continuous training they have acquired these abilities.

II. 2 Informed - *Information means power!* I must confess that the first time when heard these words I smiled maliciously. With time I have discovered that this sentence is very true and has strong significations. Why is this sentence true? Because the strongest work instrument and the most powerful advantage is information. Would you like me to give you some examples? The examples are everywhere, including in sales.

II.3 It is normal and natural that at a certain moment of your carrier you will want to be a *Team Leader*. Nothing special about this. You must be careful because this thing is possible if two essential conditions are fulfilled. First of all, you must be the best *Sales representative* of the team; secondly, you must have strong managerial abilities! I consider that it is no longer necessary to argument these affirmations. I just want to tell you that I have repeatedly used the quality of the best *Sales Representative* in order to win or in order to gain the respect and obedience (in the good sense of the word) of the subordinates. More accurately, by demonstrating them better than any of them, I have solved a great part of the situations of indiscipline or lack of subordination. In addition, this method has helped me to offer a plus of motivation and consolidation to the team.

II. 4 Long time ago, somebody has advised me to participate to many interviews, irrespective of the fact that I intention or not to accept that job. I followed his advice and I did not regret this at all. On the contrary, I recommend you to do the same. Why? First of all, because you get used to the atmosphere of these confrontations and you will eliminate the emotions inherent to them. Secondly, because you find out many things about what the employers want from their employees and you will be able to develop you capacity to fulfil correctly and in time the objectives requested by your hierarchic superiors. Thirdly, because you will gain trust in your own forces. Finally, because before learning how to sell the products and the services of the company you work in, you will learn to sell what is more important and more precious: yourself! Thus, you will learn to sell yourself correctly and accurately by exercising with the help of interviews. I guarantee you that you will have no regrets!

II.5 If you did not confront yet with the question referring to the difference between efficient and effective, sooner or later this thing will happen. From a linguistic point of view, the two terms are very close. In the context of sales the difference exists and it is strong enough. An effective agent achieves his objectives no matter what without taking into consideration the consumption of resources (effort, time, costs). An efficient agent achieves his objectives with a minimum consumption of resources. It is good to know both from the perspective of self-evaluation and self-knowledge and to the perspective of one of the hardest question of an interview.

II.6 Few suggestions of courses for you to follow in order t enlarge your knowledge: sales courses, courses of efficiency in sales, sale process, sale techniques, objections, typologies of clients, negotiation techniques, verbal and non-verbal communication, behavioural and social psychology, etc.

II.7 Filter the information you have access to or will be supplied with. In any situation, do not assimilate them without filtering them. I consider that it is useless to argument why it is good and why you must proceed in this way.

II.8 You have great care of the development of what we call generically general culture. The latter will enable you to sustain certain discussions on themes different to the act of sales. If you did not discover until now, you will certainly notice that general themes intervene in the sale process. If you do not know to interfere in this king of discussions or if you do not succeed to evade (in this case it is totally not recommended) you will have many things to lose: the ambient, disposition of the interlocutor, his relaxation which can lead to the compromising of the sale process.

II. 9 During your training, you will find out the following paradox: the more you learn, the more you will have the impression that you will have more to learn. This perception is correct! Attention! Take care not to fall on the other side. Continue your training process!

II.10 It is very important to know your company with its history and people, financial and commercial policy, products or services and competition, attributions, rights and obligations, job description, internal regulations, work procedures, objectives, targets, what you have to do every day, etc. Without all these, you cannot sell as you should. And you still have to know so many things . . .

III

The instruments of a sales agent, attitude and few suggestions related to the working manner

The instruments of a sales agent

III. 1 *Phonebook or database* - must be structured in order to enable an easier and more rapid accessibility. Divide your prospects on different categories in compliance with your necessities and objectives. I believe that it is not the case to remind you how unpleasant it is to have an urgent need of a telephone number that you do not find.

III. 2 *Presentation documents* - they represent your mirror. The documents must be impeccable, without any mark, subsequent annotations or erasing, arranged in an order, in a logic and functional succession. Imagine a date in which you do not find what you want to show or argument to the interlocutor; you have all the chances to irritate him and to compromise the date. Or worse: open the presentation file and several papers, folders begin to fall. The disaster has been produced!

III. 3 *File with activity reports* - must be organized; the easiest modality is chronological arrangement or, if applicable, on thematic of projects. I ensure you that you do not want to be in the situation in which one of you superiors ask you such a document and you do not find time it in time.

III. 4 *Observation sheets* - I recommend you to create and to work with individual observation sheets for each partner in part, in which to note the date of the meeting and the main ideas. Before the next meeting read the content of the sheet. You have in front of you the history of the discussions and implicitly a strong instrument to correct the mistakes and the omissions made. By writing your personal observations you will identify more easily your future manner of approach. I shall tell you one more tip: remember a personal detail or a particularity of your previous discussions, the interlocutor will conclude that you give him a special attention. You take great care of the interpretation of this role: if you feel that you do not know the technique of natural reactions very well, abandon this approach. Suspecting that you are artificial, your interlocutor will become circumspect and reserved.

III. 5 *Writing instrument* - First of all, your writing instrument must be clean and without any mark. Secondly, it is advisable not to be a cheap one. Within the limits of possibilities, it is advisable to be marked with the emblem, signs or particularities of the company you represent.

III. 6 *Folder or suitcase* - must be intact and clean. I hope it is clear why. In no situation, no not use bags! I will argument this recommendation by telling you briefly about en event from the beginning of my carrier. The business owner, a very pedant and extremely exigent person, firmly declared his intention to collaborate with another company requesting a meeting with its representative. The person in cause has presented at the established hour, but has left the office in ten seconds! In a state of shock I have asked my employer what happened, knowing his special interest for that business. Irritated, he answered me that he made no business with persons who came at the meeting with the documents in a bag!

III. 7 *Offers* - must contain precise, rigorous and brief information (to present only the essential). A too large material determines a decrease of the interest of the future partner for that information and reduces your role! The offers must emanate professionalism. Without stains, erasing or subsequent annotations. Without useless graphic artifices. Use sober fonts with a dimension of the characters of 12-14. If the situation allows it, present the content on one or more full pages without too large spaces.

III. 8 *Principles* - There are few self-imposed, general rules that you should comply with in any conditions and in all situations. DO NOT violate these principles if you want to be vertical persons.

III. 9 *Working system* - Create your working system that you will strictly comply with. This system is concretized by the following: DTDL (*Daily To Do List*), WDTL (*Weekly To Do List*), MTDL (*Monthly To Do List*), GTDL (*General To Do List*).

Attitude

III. 10 Adopt a positive attitude! Think positive (the force of the thought cannot be measured) and act in the same manner! Be positive even if at the beginning it will be very difficult! With time you will convince yourselves of the power of this attitude!

III. 11 The telephone contact must be short, clear and concise. Without stutters, useless breaks or too detailed information (except for the case in which you are required to develop the subject).

III. 12 The distance to the interlocutor. This aspect is described in detail and regulated in the courses of non-verbal communication. From what I have read, the recommended distance is of 1.0-1.2 m.

If the distance between you and your interlocutor is too small, the latter will have a state of discomfort or even of irritation. If this distance is too great, the message transmitted by you will dissipate and will lack intensity. Both situations lack productivity.

III. 13 Be permanently prepared to deal with unpredicted situations! It is better to act in order to avoid unpleasant situations. You agree that this thing cannot always happen, isn't it?

III. 14 Your image is your most precious business card! You must take great care not to destroy it because it will represent you your entire life.

III. 15 Language - You must use an elevated and elaborated language, a literary one, without slangs, tendentious, trivial or vulgar expressions, jargons and regionalisms.

III. 16 Position of the head - When you sit on your feet, you must have a straight position with your legs closed. When you sit down, do not relax excessively in your chair!

III. 17 The presentation - must be very clear and concise, based on very well documented and well known data, armed with indubitable and insurmountable arguments. If you are at the beginning of your carrier and you haven't still acquired security and fluency in your presentation, I recommend you to draw up and sustain the presentation in front of your friends or family. Although it seems unbelievable, the most difficult thing to do is to expose a subject in front of them. If you do not believe me, try it! After you will be convinced, continue until you will acquire fluency and coherence. Only afterwards you will be prepared to perform your presentation in front of your clients.

III. 18 Sincerity - Make use of it to a certain extent, Please do not understand that I suggest you to lie. This is not my intention! I just want to say that it is better that you know certain things.

Each person will analyse what and how much enters this category of information.

III. 19 Conduct - clean, common and functional. Without extravagant haircuts, without accessories in excess. Men must shave regularly. I am convinced that I do not need to offer other details.

III. 20 Make use correctly and carefully of the goods of the company! Mainly, because these goods are not yours (you have the moral duty to respect the work of your colleagues), but also because in this way you will demonstrate that you are responsible persons.

III. 21 Clothes - The best solution seems to be the classical suit, in dark or warm (during summer) colours, without strident nuances. It is not acceptable to wear a neck opening or a shirt without a tie. In one word: you must be business. At one of my previous jobs, the shirt without a tie was allowed (black shoes and classic pans were compulsory) at temperatures above 30°C. Lack of compliance with these norms led to the cancellation of the employment contract.

Few suggestions related to the working manner

III. 22 Automatism kills creativity! That is why it is indicated to alternate routine activities with dynamic ones which stress you continuously.

III. 23 You have a problem and you do not know how to solve it or you are in a situation with no exit. This thing does not exist! If even after you have requested somebody's help you have no solution, I recommend you to dedicate to a routine activity (filling in of sheets, reports, study of a material, etc.), allowing in this way the sedimentation of the information. If you have thought intensely to that subject and have exhausted all the approaches, a solution surely will come (I repeat: it will seem that the solution came alone;

in reality it is the consequence of a complex phenomenon of analysis and synthesis of the human brain) after a certain period. These are the explanation and the mechanism of "sleep inventions".

III. 24 When you ask for favours (exclusively related to the present or possible future collaboration) to your interlocutors, if you want to force a little the establishment of a meeting or if you want to determine the concretization (pronunciation) of a decision, try the following formulation: "I want to ask you to . . .". The use of this formulation will be perceived by your interlocutor as a sign of security and self-control. Test it and decide for yourselves.

III. 25 The orders are negotiable, they are not transcribed. This is the difference between a sales agent and a scribe—each of them has abilities specific to the trade or occupation.

III. 26 If you are nervous during the meeting keep your hands together. In this way, you will hide your fear and will acquire trust in your own forces. More than this, your interlocutors will not observe your weakness and will no longer have the occasion to explore it, in the sense of creating a conjuncture advantage.

III. 27 If your interlocutor does not grant sufficient attention to your exposal or if he is preoccupied by his own problems, stop, make a significant break of few seconds (until he will get out from the state of indifference) and start the presentation again. The effect is guaranteed!

III. 28 If you did not safety in speaking on the phone, write down the text of your presentation. In this way you will avoid stutters and with time you will gain fluency in conversation. I ensure you that soon you will no longer need that piece of paper. It is n extremely simple method to stimulate the trust in your person.

III. 29 Asian philosophy indicates three valences of the opinions, not two as in the case of European philosophy. Thee valences include:

yes (to choose), no (not to choose) and another opinion which is strictly personal and nobody knows it (lack of choosing). Please do not conclude that I suggest you to be hypocrite or false. This is not my intention! It is in your own interest to filter the information that you supply!

III. 30 White sheet of paper - it is an extremely efficient modality to draw and to gain the attention of the interlocutor. By concretizing the explanations by means of graphic elements you determine your interlocutor to follow your judgment or presentation. It is worthy to try this method the moment when the other person has lost the line of your explanations: "Yes, yes . . ."

III. 31 The interlocutor requires a cancellation of the meeting and asks you to call him again next week, Monday or Tuesday, for example. Tell him that you will call him on Tuesday at the established hour. This choice denotes the fact that you are relaxed and you are not desperate to initiate new partnerships.

III. 32. Finally, after you have established the date and hour of your following meeting, write down in front of your interlocutor in your agenda all these dates. Besides the absolutely necessary organization character of this action, there three more aspects: 1. Your interlocutor will make the same fact which decreases drastically the chances for the next meeting not to take place; 2. You will eliminate in this way the chances to establish two meetings with different persons at the same hour; 3. The person in cause will appreciate the fact that you offer her a great attention.

III. 33 Keep carefully all the information collected and important ideas! At a certain moment, you will definitely need them.

III. 34 Personal evaluation system - Why is this system necessary? For the self-evaluation of the activity and for a periodic monitoring of the performances. It is the only valid method to correct the mistakes.

III. 35 Establish clear objectives, measurable indicators and well defined deadlines. Only in this way, you can turn competitive!

III. 36 You will be late or you will not attend a meeting (in exception cases, but this must not become a rule), for reasons independent by your will. Call your interlocutor and announce him to wait for you if he can or to reschedule the meeting. It is the only correct modality to act in this situation!

IV

The relation with your interlocutors

IV.1 Help your colleagues! I recommend you to do this not only from the perspective of the exchange, but mainly for *fair play* and collegiality reasons.

IV.2 When somebody who does not have the authority to trace duties he does so, look warmly in his eyes and smile. He will disarm and review his attitude.

IV.3 Ask for help when you are in trouble! Spare precious time and a lot of energy in this way. In addition, the sender of the request, colleague or hierarchic superior will appreciate the fact that you have chosen him to offer an advice, an opinion, a recommendation, etc.

IV.4 Ask for the permission to address to your hierarchic superior of your boss when you have a problem that your *Team Leader* cannot or does not have the competence to solve it! This thing must happen after your superior has been informed on that situation and has confirmed that he cannot help you. Otherwise, the person in cause will lose the trust in you and will consider that you doubt his competence or, worse will conclude that you want to undermine his authority. Any of these situations are very dangerous and generate big trouble.

IV.5 Communication is the only way in our path towards success. Why? Because by means of communication we eliminate obstacles, irrespective of their nature. By communicating, we come up with new ideas which enable the process of finding a solution to different problems. That is why, several symposiums, conferences, congresses are organized; for the same reason (exchange of ideas) *brainstorming* meetings are held.

IV.6 How do you determine your interlocutor to pay you attention if he is busy or if he wants to test your patience a little? Fix him with your eyes right into the point located at the half of the distance between the eyes. In few minutes he will feel that you supervise him and will stop his previous activity and pay you the attention you need. This thing does not mean that he will not be less embarrassed by this situation which offers you an advantage because that person will give up the arrogance. Just try!

IV.7 Be very careful to the relations with your interlocutors who do not look into your eyes or who do not have the strength to sustain your regard! These are hidden persons from whom you can expect to everything. I refer especially to unpleasant surprises which is better to be avoided!

IV.8 Inform your hierarchic superiors on the negative aspects that you discover in the activity of the department or of the company, but without changing the sense of the information and without accusing somebody! As a result of this action, nobody must have troubles! It is important that the person or competent persons to know the truth, to take the measures imposed and to solve these situations in everybody's interest and not to somebody's detriment.

IV.9 The most frequent objections which appear as a result of the request for a meeting are the following: "I do not want to", "I cannot", "I do not have time", "I am not interested", etc. In most of the cases, you can demount these objections by using the following formula: "It is hard for me to believe that you are not interested in . . ." and continue with something important for your interlocutor. It is obvious that this solution supposes to know the sensitive and/or essential elements for the person you speak with.

IV.10 The paradox of the communication is the following: the person who speaks less leads the discussion. The person who speaks more develops, under a form or another, his intentions, needs, strengths and weaknesses. This is very precious information for a sales agent if he knows to recognize and to use this information. Thus, speak less and listen more!

IV.11 Politeness - represents the transposition in facts and attitude of good manners, so necessary in day to day life.

IV.12 Look your interlocutors right in the eyes! In this way you will observe their most hidden reactions and with little training you will be able to anticipate their tactic movements. Certainly, it is not easy to proceed as such, but you can, if you are able to hold yourself dominate them (in the good and constructive sense of the word)! In addition, they will perceive you as a strong person and will offer you both their trust and the respect necessary to certain collaboration or partnership relations. This thing is valid in the case of people who have verticality; otherwise, they do not deserve to waste time. A relation based on solid principles, of collaboration brings more benefits than ten false relations!

IV.13 Answer to all the hellos addressed to you even if for the moment you do not recognize that person! Reacting in this way you will respect yourself! Otherwise, at the next meeting, the interlocutor will behave in a manner which you will not enjoy. The relation is compromised!

IV.14 Respect the truth! The necessity of this advice can be the object of a wide paper which at this moment I am not prepared to elaborate. It is certain still that we must not deviate from this rule, no matter what!

IV.15 Respect the hierarchy of the department and of the company. This hierarchy is not established by chance and has the role to define the competences and the limits of each employee. Without order and discipline the evolution and the well being of everybody is absolutely impossible! If the employees do not respect the hierarchy, they will generate disorder and chaos!

IV.16 Comply with the rules and the laws! It is the only correct modality to develop your activity, irrespective of the fact that you agree or do not agree with their provisions. If you have any observations in relation to the amendments, modifications or improvements, you are free to do it. It is no less true that the importance of the manner in which you do it: tactically (in order not to hurt somebody's authority) and only based on arguments! Until the moment when new regulations will be operated, strictly comply with what is in operation at that moment! It is the easiest way of action, keeps you away from troubles and enables you to consume minimum resources!

IV.17 Respect your interlocutors (partners, superiors, colleagues, etc.)! In this way you demonstrate that you respect yourself!

IV.18 It happens frequently enough to require repeatedly a meeting and to receive the following answer: "I will cal you . . ." In case you are not sure that your interlocutor does not want or even cannot meet with you, you can elucidate the mystery by using the following question: "Is this a polite way of telling me not to cal you again?" Attention: this formula presents the risk of irritating the interlocutor!

IV.19 A question has been addressed to you and you still need few seconds to formulate the correct answer which advantages you. How will you get out of this situation? A possible solution is to reply: "I am afraid that I have not understood your question very well". While your interlocutor reformulates the question, structure the response wanted.

V

What not to do . . .

V.1 DO NOT abandon when you are in difficulty! Reanalyze the situation and persevere! This is the adequate attitude of a sales agent.

V.2 DO NOT accept a promotion with your eyes closed! Evaluate correctly your chances and potential and be sure that you are prepared for a new activity. Otherwise, the failure will be disastrous.

V.3 DO NOT accept any job; as the employers reserve the right to select you or not, you are entitled to choose the company you want to represent.

V.4 DO NOT accept a job in which all the aspects of the collaboration are not very well defined: rights and obligations, sales history and objectives, measurable indicators of performance and perspectives!

V.5 DO NOT act negatively, but progressively! Nobody prefers or should not prefer regress instead of progress.

V.6 DO NOT act at random! DO NOT work at random, but according to a plan! Nothing is less productive than a chaotic activity, with no order and clear steps.

V.7 DO NOT hide the unpleasant (inconvenient) aspects of the collaboration! Give it an acceptable form but necessarily with accent on reality in the spirit of the truth!

V.8 DO NOT expect more than 15 minutes for the partner or the future partner to come! Your time is as precious as his time. Teach him to respect you! In a week (or sooner) call him and start talking with this kind of phrase: "We did not manage to meet last week. I want to ask you to . . ." In this way, you are not annoying (as a result of the insistency) and you have obtained a slight advantage on the interlocutor who is in difficulty.

V.9 DO NOT expect for rewards! Act to receive them as a result of the activity and of your results, and not as result of the efforts made to obtain those benefits. Work correctly and the rewards will come. It depends only on you to identify them. And something else: you must be patient; these pleasant surprises do not appear immediately. DO NOT request or pretend something more (praises, merits, benefits)! Sooner or later, under one form or another, you will have to return them, a behaviour which is not very easy or pleasant. In addition, this kind of behaviour contravenes to professional ethics.

V.10 DO NOT wait to happen something you want! Take action!

V.11 DO NOT fall in the extreme of countless diplomas!

V.12 DO NOT fall in anonymity! There is a natural tendency, in the stage where you are not very sure on the luggage of knowledge and you are not aware of the potential you have, to feel that you must not come out in front of your colleagues. I shall argument this recommendation by telling you briefly a situation I met at one of my first jobs. I was participating to the national sales meeting with all the representatives of area. Each representative was analysed in the presence of all his colleagues by the leading body (General Manager and National Sales Manager) from the perspective of the results obtained in the previous year. When it came the turn of another colleague who was at the half of the classification the General Manager said: "I never heard anything about you—good or bad. Write your resignation. Shocking, isn't it?"

V.13 DO NOT consume alcoholic drinks during your working schedule! Nothing or almost nothing is more disturbing for the interlocutor than a representative who smells like alcohol! You have the responsibility not to bring any prejudice to the company you represent!

V.14 DO NOT develop two different activities in parallel! You will lose your focus which will reflect in a decrease of the level of performance and implicitly of the results. You can be good or very good only in one field of activity! Chose this field and remain faithful to it!

V.15 DO NOT avoid parties! They constitute an excellent mean to disconnect and to socialize.

V.16 DO NOT hesitate a *role play!* Their scope is to train you for the real situations in which you confront your interlocutors and not between your colleagues.

V.17 DO NOT exaggerate with your labour in the detriment of your health and family! Jobs are everywhere . . .

V.18 DO NOT execute the dispositions received without filtering them in your thoughts!

V.19 DO NOT make compromises! DO NOT deviate from your principles! DO NOT forget the rules of a good education! Apply them!

V.20 DO NOT make the mistake to neglect your activity even if you intend or follow to change your job! Make your duty and fulfil with your obligations until the last minute of the contract. This is the way in which it is good and you should proceed.

V.21 DO NOT make the mistake to neglect your job not even the moment when you are sure that you will change the company! Make your duty until the end of the last contractual day! There are two reasons for which I recommend this thing: 1. unpleasant surprises can appear anytime, irrespective if you expect them or you are prepared to treat them as such or not; 2. This attitude is in accordance with the required professional ethics and with the professionalism towards which you must tend.

V.22 DO NOT make false (unfounded) promises! If you are not sure that you can do what you said you would do, it is better not to promise. A false promise will definitely bring you the lack of consideration of your interlocutor.

V.23 DO NOT deviate from the ethics and from your professional conduct! For nothing in the world!

V.24 DO NOT be aggressive in language and behaviour! Aggressiveness, so damaging and lacking recommendation in any field, is characteristic for the persons whose professional training is precarious.

V.25 DO NOT be artificial (other than usual). Be natural! Both the naturalness and the lack of naturalness are extremely easy to perceive.

V.26 DO NOT be generically neuter because not always neutrality is the best tactics. There are situations in which it is better and you must adopt a firm and decisive attitude, pro or against.

V.27 DO NOT be refractory to the changes meant to improve your activity! Even if these changes suppose an additional study or the modification of the work system.

V.28 DO NOT feel tensioned, be relaxed! DO NOT be passive, be active! DO NOT be isolated, be open!

V.29 DO NOT be more exigent than you should with yourselves, but only as required!

V.30 DO NOT behave like slaves or arrogant!

V.31 DO NOT use expressions such as "if you want", "if you can" because in this way you will open evading channels that your partner will use to block you or to delay your actions and intentions!

V.32 DO NOT use the conditional form of the verb (I would like)! This structure denotes uncertainty and lack of trust in your own forces, attitudes which any interlocutor with a certain experience will exploit in your disfavour.

V.33 DO NOT use excessively artifices specific to the act of sale because you will risk degrading the basic message!

V.34 DO NOT use closed questions except for the situations in which you are sure of the answer! The surest modality is to use open questions with guided response which will be of a real help in obtaining the finality desired. I recommend these methods to the ones who have a considerable experience because in these cases it is very easy to make mistakes that the interlocutor will be able to use in your disfavour.

V.35 DO NOT use the name of the company in your own interest because you are not entitled to!

V.36 DO NOT formulate judgments on situations which you are not entitled to evaluate or you are not prepared to do it! The interlocutors will not see with good eyes these interventions and certainly they will not be appreciated.

V.37 DO NOT formulate a too long introduction before transmitting an unpleasant message! You will only emphasize the state of discomfort of your interlocutor.

V.38 DO NOT smoke if your interlocutor is not smoking! Not even if he allows you to smoke! You create a state of discomfort which will certainly bring damages to the future (potential) relation.

V.39 DO NOT generate conflicts and make all your efforts in order to avoid them! These conflicts are great consumers of resources and attract an entire series of troubles. Follow your path!

V.40 DO NOT make excessive gestures or too large movements because these actions induce a state of nervousness to the interlocutor!

V.41 DO NOT "invent" what has already been invented!

V.42 DO NOT force the interlocutors to decide! Make them decide!

V.43 DO NOT begin the sentences with "No!" The word "Nu!" used at the beginning of the sentence induces a refractory, refuse attitude to the interlocutor.

V.44 DO NOT try to know your interlocutor before knowing yourselves!

V.45 DO NOT try to make all sympathize you because you will not succeed! This is a warranty!

V.46 DO NOT try to ask, if applicable "what?", "how?", "why?", "when?", etc! Think of the duties you are entrusted with. I want to ask you to understand that I do not suggest you to lack subordination (This is not my intention!) but I recommend you not to execute without thinking. Let's not forget that we are human beings and we have the possibility to think.

V.47 DO NOT end the day before finalizing everything you have proposed to do! If you used to let things unsolved, you will find out soon that you have many things to do than in a usual day. I am extremely curious how you will solve this problem. More than this, one part of the situations wouldn't have appeared subsequently if you had solved them when you had to. Nobody is obliged to fulfil with your job duties and nobody will do it.

V.48 DO NOT deliberately delay the fulfilment of job duties! There are other factors which will cause delays irrespective if you want or not.

V.49 DO NOT be late at work! Strictly comply with your work schedule!

V.50 DO NOT lay "traps" if you are not sure that your interlocutor will fall! It's exactly as playing with the fire! It burns!

V.51 DO NOT perform actions without a detailed previous training! It is at least pathetic the intervention of a sales agent who does not have accurate information and who works at random. DO NOT neglect the report activity/results! If you act according to the rules and you have an intense activity, you will obtain the desired results!

V.52 DO NOT brutally interrupt your interlocutor! It is impolite from your part and frustrating for him. Introduce your replies tactfully so that, even you do not speak much, you transmit the message.

V.53 DO NOT interrupt the exposure and presentation of the superior because the break has arrived! There are few cases in which you will not suggest antipathy by acting in this way.

V.54 DO NOT deliberately let small doors by means of which the interlocutor will be able to surprise you; otherwise, he will have the opportunity to take control.

V.55 DO NOT let the offers to analyse them later (it is one of the classic evading methods of the possible buyers)! In most of the cases, these offers will arrive to garbage! Discuss them, present them and argument them!

V.56 DO NOT let the interlocutors observe that you treat them with indifference! In this way, you will only incite their self-pride which is extremely dangerous for you activity.

V.57 DO NOT miss the meetings within the department or the company! Even if you consider them boring and useless, you are wrong. In this way you will non-verbally express the affiliation to the collective and you have the real possibility to find out new things which will help you in your activity.

V.58 DO NOT take rapid decision! You will make fun of yourselves and will create many problems. This recommendation is valid both for personal situations and for the professional ones. First analyze than act!

V.59 DO NOT have a break in the present of your hierarchic superiors! The gesture can be interpreted as ostentatious, lack of respect, etc. Except for the situations in which hours of the breaks are regulated in the Interior Regulation Policy.

V.60 DO NOT eat or chew during the meeting! It is very impolite for your interlocutor.

V.61 DO NOT go to work only to have somewhere to come from! If you are not capable and you show no will to develop your activity within normal parameters, take a day off. You can ruin many things if you work with no mood. Take care not to become a custom!

V.62 DO NOT work without thinking! We all know what catastrophes derive from this practice.

V.63 DO NOT neglect arguments! On the contrary, please do not waste any opportunity (presentation, exposal, verbal duel—in the good sense of the word, etc.) to use them. Any other method is unsuitable to a sales agent.

V.64 DO NOT neglect the interests and the wishes of the partners/interlocutors! They are the source of the sale; only by exploring them we can sell.

V.65 DO NOT neglect the message besides words! It is so easy to speak in this way because it offers extremely important information.

V.66 DO NOT communicate offers by telephone! Not even professional sellers do not act this way very often because a correct and complete sale will be obtained when we will explore all the resources (needs, intentions, reactions, objections, etc) which are possible only by means of a face to face discussion. The only thing that you must do is to incite his interest, to determine your interlocutor to want to meet with you.

V.67 DO NOT ever omit to defend and ask for your rights! You must know your rights, and the way in which you ask for them must be polite and civilized. To an equal extent, you must be very well informed on your job attributions, duties and obligations.

V.68 DO NOT forget to test your interlocutors from time to time (in relation to their interest, fidelity, etc.)! If they test you, you should do the same.

V.69 DO NOT forget the fact that the most important values of a company are the human ones. Act in such a manner to be considered one of these values!

V.70 DO NOT forget for a second which are your advantages and defects!

V.71 DO NOT waste any opportunity to transform NO in YES!

V.72 DO NOT forget what, to whom and how you sell!

V.73 DO NOT discuss in excess! You will waste energy and time which are extremely precious in your activity. Focus on really important things: activity, objectives and results.

V.74 DO NOT report erroneously! What you will report will influence the decisions taken by your superiors; if you do not report correctly, the decisions will be wrong (unrealistic) and will negatively influence your activity. This is why Murphy advices us to stay away from GIGO effect.

V.75 DO NOT laugh loud! It is impolite and deranging!

V.76 DO NOT represent two competitive companies at the same time! (see I.8, I.11 and I. 17). You will have big troubles if one of the companies will accuse of disloyal competition. Moreover, if the company requires damages for image, you will leave them as inheritance to your nephews!

V.77 DO NOT change the proportion of 90%—10% between arguments and *pressing*! If the arguments have a lower rate, the sale is incorrectly and incompletely performed; with time, this situation will be seen by everybody.

V.78 DO NOT change a working system which functions! This is one of the basic management rules. If a method leads to results, improve it, do not change it!

V.79 DO NOT shorten your meetings without justification! DO NOT extend your meetings unless necessary! Both situations are deranging for the interlocutors.

V.80 DO NOT sign any document (job description, employment contract, fidelity contract, etc.) without a previous detail study of that document. What is written will remain written and you cannot subsequently excuse saying that you did not know.

V.81 DO NOT ask for help just to do it (in order to enter somebody's graces, to make yourself remarked or to aliment somebody's ego), but only when you really need that help!

V.82 DO NOT ask for personal favours to your interlocutors! You will lose the equal position you have, Please believe me that you do not want this.

V.83 DO NOT require recommendations from the first meeting! Wait until the relation will be created and will be stable, until the interlocutor trusts you. In my opinion, it is suitable to ask for recommendations after the signing of the collaboration contract.

I guarantee you that at that moment the reserve to supply recommendations is nearly zero!

V.84 DO NOT say "Thank you" for your salary unless you are absolutely sure you deserve it!

V.85 DO NOT establish meetings at the end of the week for the beginning of the next week! In a proportion of 90% the interlocutor will forget (except for the situations in which you are convinced that he has written down the date).

V.86 DO NOT undermine under any circumstances the authority of the superiors!

V.87 DO NOT over-dimension the orders (deliberately and without the written consent of the interlocutor)! It is unprofessional and I ensure you that the second time you will no longer have the opportunity to do it at the same buyer-partner. When other people will find out (sooner or later the inevitable will produce) that you make use of this kind of practices ("tune" style), you will lose any collaboration. If you do not succeed to sell what and how much you want, stop selling!

V.88 DO NOT forget which are the greatest enemies of a sales agent: ignorance and time. The lack of knowledge will not be absolved by mistakes. Never. Time is passing in you disfavour. Always.

V.89 DO NOT forget that the basis of the relations between companies is ensured by the relations between their representatives! You will represent the employer in everything you will do. You should act accordingly!

V.90 DO NOT forget that the best defence is the attack! In the most pacifist sense of the expression.

V.91 DO NOT forget that perfection will be achieved only by exercise.

V.92 DO NOT forget that there are always multiple options! It depend on you what you choose!

V.93 DO NOT forget that people are not equal! I do not refer to rights, but to possibilities.

V.94 DO NOT forget that in order to be chosen by your partners (for collaboration), you must make the remark you in the good sense of the word.

V.95 DO NOT forget that you are the engine and the lance of the company because you produce money! Behave as such!

V.96 DO NOT forget that you are integral part of the compartment or department. Behave as such without discordant attitudes or actions which might bring prejudices to your colleagues. If you have the opportunity and possibility bring improvements or propose optimizations of the activity of your team. DO NOT forget any moment that in everything you do you are the representative of the company! I am convinced that you know that negative actions are much easier and much longer retained than positive ones and that you have heard at least one time remarks such as "Look what X from Y company did". Consequently, you have the responsibility to maintain and to defend the image of the company.

V.97 DO NOT forget that certain products or services are sold, they are not bought! In these cases, the approach is totally different starting inevitably from inducing and stimulation of the needs of interlocutors and not from exploring their declared intentions.

V.98 DO NOT forget that the sale begins from the first second of the interaction with you interlocutor! Any wrong action or remark can compromise everything.

V.99 DO NOT forget any moment your goals and objectives! Do everything you need to achieve them!

V.100 DO NOT forget to ask for the feed-back of your actions! IT is one of the only palpable modalities to self-evaluate you.

V.101 DO NOT forget to be tolerant! We all make mistakes. More important and more correct is to be exigent with ourselves.

V.102 DO NOT forget to leave your business card, to ask the telephone number of your interlocutor, to fix the date of the next meeting, etc! All these mistakes will affect your activity; in order to obtain this date you will lose precious time!

V.103 DO NOT forget to thank for the help received, for the time and for the meeting, etc!

V.104 DO NOT forget to apologize when you have committed a mistake! This thing is very important both from the perspective of the correctness towards own person and from the perspective of the correctness towards your interlocutors. Moreover, the action must be sincere, not formal and conjectural.

V.105 DO NOT forget to treat your interlocutors as special persons!

V.106 DO NOT forget to congratulate your clients for their birthdays or other significant occasions for them (see III.1, III.4).

V.107 DO NOT forget to write down all the coordinates of the meeting (date, hour, exact address, etc.) from the first telephone. It is very deranging for your interlocutor to call him and to ask for additional clarifications. This attitude denotes lack of interest from your part and degrades the collaboration relations.

V.108 DO NOT forget to check the existence of the partner' signature on the contract, request, order, etc. When you come back for these reasons there is the possibility to have unpleasant surprises.

V.109 DO NOT forget to smile! The smile is the easiest and the most pleasant modality to open the channels of inter-human communication so necessary in daily activities. To an equal extent, the smile is a very powerful weapon: the smile will get us out of trouble.

V.110 DO NOT use the goods of the company but in its own interest and in no situation in your personal interest! Their role is to facilitate the achievement of the professional objectives and not to solve your personal problems.

V.111 DO NOT use words whose sense you do not know! You have great chances to make big mistakes, sometimes irreversible, which will affect your image and your results implicitly.

V.112 DO NOT use the term "client" in excess! It is perceived as being too commercial in the detriment of inter-human relations. When possible, replace this term with "partner" or "interlocutor" if, in this way you will not change the sense and the destination of the message.

V.113 DO NOT use materials with the signs of the competition (pens, briquettes, agendas, etc.)! It is possible that your interlocutor formulate an uncomfortable question to which you have no answer.

V.114 DO NOT use, in your exposures, "hard" sentences! There is the risk that both you and your interlocutor lose the basic idea (valid especially for beginners). There are also derogations from this rule, when you deliberately want to "capture" your interlocutor. In this case you should comply with a compulsory condition: to master this technique very well because otherwise you risk failing to obtain the finality desires and to be ridiculous. That is why I recommend this practice to the most experimented ones.

V.115 DO NOT desperately accept any meeting which cannot take place in good conditions from client's fault (you are at his office and the discussion is repeatedly interrupted by external interventions)! You request the re-schedule of the meeting at a subsequent date. Your interlocutor will perceive this action as the one of a professional who pays him the required attention, who does not act randomly, but wants to build a real and sustainable partner.

V.116 DO NOT engage in discussions on themes you do not know! You have great chances to become ridiculous or even hilarious. You can participate as passive part who listens.

V.117 DO NOT rely only on memory! For different reasons (tiredness, stress, etc.) you can forget the most important aspects of your activity!

V.118 DO NOT rely exclusively on intuition!

V.119 DO NOT gossip your colleagues, superiors or company! It is unprofessional and will bring you absolutely no benefits. In addition, there is the possibility that your interlocutor does not consider you a trustful person and to show no interest in your collaboration.

V.120 DO NOT enjoy and DO NOT benefit from somebody else's trouble!

V.121 DO NOT exceed your competence limits! Extend them by professional development!

V.122 DO NOT make a rule from answering questions with questions! You will be catalogued as "sleepy", lacking trust.

V.123 DO NOT stay away from periodic testing (theoretic or practical)! They have the role of maintaining a high level of knowledge.

V.124 DO NOT guide after the expression "it works this way"! Good things are not made at random and performance cannot appear in any conditions!

V.125 DO NOT guide after the expression "this cannot happen to me"! It can happen to anybody! I refer strictly to unpleasant events.

V.126 DO NOT hurry! Solve the problems calmly, after a careful and detailed analysis in order to avoid mistakes. Good things are made in a relaxing manner! Always.

V.127 DO NOT involve in the problems of your interlocutors! These stories are intended to hide the reserves they have in relation to your collaboration. Identify the objections and dismount them!

V.128 DO NOT let negativist persons to impede you! Stay away from them!

V.129 DO NOT oppose to the intentions/attempts of the interlocutors to test you! If this thing is in your advantage, let them test you!

V.130 DO NOT launch affirmations without covering (without a fundament)! You will be classified as a person whose words are not reliable which is extremely unpleasant.

V.131 DO NOT let you influenced and directed towards unproductive finalities! DO NOT allow your interlocutor to lead the discussion! DO NOT let your interlocutor lead you!

V.132 DO NOT let you conquered by emotions! Control them and be their master!

V.133 DO NOT praise your luggage of knowledge, with the information you hold or with the relations you have. Use them!

V.134 DO NOT be intimidated by difficult interlocutors! Imagine them in a hilarious position and you will discover that they are o longer unapproachable.

V.135 DO NOT limit only to the theoretic preparation or only to the practical one; one without the other are incomplete. Approach afferent fields also!

V.136 DO NOT limit only to one strategy! There is also the possibility that your interlocutor knows or worse guesses you strategy and dismounts it. You do not want this to happen believe me! Consequently, you should think of many strategies and use them to the same extent. In this way, you can play with them changing the path when the situation asks for this change; the chances of success will increase as the possibility of failure will decrease.

V.137 DO NOT ever neglect your job! This is your source of existence and you must take great care of it. It depends on you how you will manage this source!

V.138 DO NOT park your car on the parking place of your manager! Should I argument? I am sure that you do need any arguments.

V.139 DO NOT allow you the mistake to commit a mistake!

V.140 DO NOT use too many details! The message transmitted must be short, clear and concise and not to be lost or altered. This thing is especially valid the moment when you want to put an end to a stage or to underline certain conclusions.

V.141 DO NOT complain to your interlocutors in relation to your troubles or dissatisfactions irrespective if they are personal or professional! There is always the possibility to sympathize you which probably will not help you with anything and your interlocutor will not consider you a reliable competitor.

V.142 DO NOT pretend to work when your employer pretend to pay you! Continue working because first of all you work for you and than for him! Take all the measures in this sense!

V.143 DO NOT pretend to work in the presence of your hierarchic superiors! Work truly, and not only for the sake of working!

V.144 DO NOT change your job before balancing the positive and negative aspect from the past, present and future! Pay a special attention to the analysis of perspectives!

V.145 DO NOT excuse in excess and with no reason (except for the case in which you are guilty)! Excuses will accuse you!

V.146 DO NOT be stressed without a reason! Leave things evolve alone!

V.147 DO NOT underestimate your opponents/competitors! They exist and you do not have to forget this aspect because your activity is influenced to a certain extent by their activity.

V.148 DO NOT underestimate you! It will destroy motivation; this state has severe negative influences on the activity performances.

V.149 DO NOT overestimate you! You will conclude that you are the best which can be very dangerous and can destroy your judgment.

V.150 DO NOT fear the questions of the interlocutor! Enjoy his questions! The fact that he requires certain information from you and that he participates actively to the discussion demonstrates that you have gained his interest and attention. You are on a great road.

V.151 DO NOT fear to ask what you do not know! It is a normal situation; except for the information supplied by the company under the form of a course or of a training material. In this case, you should ask only what you haven's understood (after a careful individual study) because you risk to receive a short answer and namely that here are aspects you should have known.

V.152 DO NOT fear to recognize that you do not know (except for compulsory information)! In this case, sincerity is appreciated. You should discuss that subject than to speak about something you do not know. Listen and learn!

V.153 DO NOT fear to refuse or to say NO! It denotes safety and character strength and self-control. It will attract the respect of the interlocutor even if he does not agree with your opinion; elegantly, tactically and with arguments.

V.154 DO NOT fear to say "I do not know" (see II.1)! Obligatorily, this remark must be followed by "I will inform and tomorrow I will offer you the answer", provided that you supply the information requested in time (otherwise you have compromised the relation built until that moment). At the same time, you can call somebody (in front of your partner will have a great impact) who will surely offer you the information; if you do not succeed in this way, turn to the first variant. In this way you have acquired a credit of trust from the part of your partner. This strategy can be used in your activity as a method of winning the trust of your interlocutor if you are absolutely sure that the mimics will not betray you.

V.155 DO NOT fear to expose and to sustain your own opinions regarding the optimization of the department or of the company! Attention: this recommendation is valid with the remark that you must be very careful to the formulation in order not to hurt the pride of a colleague or worse, the authority of a hierarchic superior!

V.156 DO NOT "treat" your interlocutors equally but take into consideration their potential! I want to make myself understood I refer strictly to the time allotted to everybody! DO NOT forget that your efficiency, productivity and capacity depend on the way in which you maintain the relations with these partners.

V.157 DO NOT sell characteristics, but benefits! DO NOT sell in a general way! Be special!

V.158 DO NOT sell what you want, but what the interlocutor needs! This recommendation is addressed strictly to those who have a small experience in sales. In order to sell what you want you must go through few stages of professional development until the level of *Senior Salesman*.

V.159 DO NOT sell to those who do not need your products or services! You only must identify the ones who make part of this category in order to be able to exclude them from your activity plans.

V.160 DO NOT sell from the first meeting! Still, if you will succeed to do it, this thing will happen thanks to luck, and not to the science.

Identify first the needs of the client in order to perform a complete and good sale.

V.161 DO NOT sell a product or a service that you do not know very well or whose benefit/utility you do not believe in! Why? Because it is less probable to obtain notable results and performances (I address especially to the one who have little experience). If you do not believe me (although for your sake you better believe me), try. After you will become "mercenaries" in sales, the situation will change; at that moment you will be able to sell everything and in any conditions. Until that stage you will have to cross a long way.

V.162 NO words, but facts! NO words, but documents! NO suppositions, but arguments!

V.163 DO NOT speak with no sense and just to speak! It is very unproductive.

V.164 DO NOT talk too loud or too slow! First of all, you will only aggress your interlocutor, and secondly you will induce him a state of discomfort or stress. Both situations cause damages (unproductive) to your activity.

Think and act, behave and be real SALESPERSONS!

VI

Instead of bibliography

The ideas exposed and developed in this paper have countered in time as a result of the interaction with the following persons (colleagues, partners, friends and hierarchic superiors):

Ioan Andriesei, Constantin Anton, Gheorghe Cristian Belcic, Doinea Benea, Tiberiu Boldur, Oliver Botez, Ioan Budeanu, Ciprian Caia, Ionuţ Carpen, Ionuţ Chiriac, Cătălin Chirvase, Cristian Colotelo, Ionuţ Crega, Iulian Dumitriu, Călin Filipescu, Viorel Goraş, Cristian Ioan, Cătălin Jolobceastăi, Dan Mancaş, Mihaela Munteanu, Liviu Nistoran, Constantin Oană, Cristian Obreja, Ionel Onofraş, Anca Paşcovici, Radu Mircea Pentie, Maria Nelli Petre, Florin Pleşescu, Gabriel Popescu, Traian Popovici, Gabriel Simion, Ionuţ Tanasă, Mihnea Theodorescu, Kostas Tsolos, Alin Zaharia.

Thank you.

For the ones who would like to formulate observations to this paper, I kindly ask them to send me their suggestions to the following address: *iulius.grosu@vitalaire.de*